Regionalisation and Interregionalism in a Post-globalisation and Post-American era

Xuan Loc Doan

February 2010

About the Author

Xuan Loc Doan is a Research Associate on Asia Programme at the Global Policy Institute. He is currently completing a PhD thesis on *Interregionalism and ASEAN-EU interaction as an example of interregionalism*. Xuan Loc Doan has written a GPI Policy Paper on *Challenges facing ASEAN and East Asia in a turbulent time* and a number of articles on international affairs which have been published on the website of Vietnamese BBC World Service.

Regionalisation and Interregionalism in a Post-globalisation and Post-American Era

1. Introduction: The emergence of regional actor in the global system

It is widely believed that the world is witnessing a series of profound social, economic and political transformations. Chief among these is the rise of new major powers, such as Brazil, Russia, India and particularly China (the 'BRICS'), which are enjoying impressive economic growth and are making a major impact on the world economy (see Table 1). Their rise is bringing about a power shift in the global system, in which power is increasingly moving away from the United States of America (US) to multiple centres. Even though remaining the world's biggest economy, the US 'is beginning to show signs of strains, particularly in some

Table 1: The four emerging powers, Brazil, Russia, India and China (BRICs)

	Population (2009)		GDP (2009)		Merchandise Trade	
	Million	%	$ billlion	%	$ billion	%
World	**6,437.8**	**100.0**	**68,651.5**	**100.0**	**28,194.0**	**100.0**
Brazil	194.4	3.0	1,973.6	2.9	287.6	1.0
Russia	141.4	2.2	2,145.8	3.3	578.6	2.1
India	1,207.5	18.8	3,469.1	5.0	362.3	1.3
China	1,334.3	20.7	8,511.1	12.1	2,174.0	7.7
Total	**2,877.6**	**44.7**	**16,099.6**	**23.3**	**3,402.5**	**12.1**

Sources: *World Economic Outlook Database*, IMF 2009;
International Trade Statistic, WTO 2008

key sectors, such as finance and banking'.[1] Put simply, 'while the US remains the most powerful country in the world, the rest of the world is catching up'.[2] This is confirmed by the recent report of the US's National Intelligence Council, which predicted that the US's role as the sole superpower would be challenged and it would become more of a 'first among equals' with the emergence of powers such as China, India and Russia.[3] That is, we are witnessing the arrival of a post-American world, not because the US is declining but because the rest are rising.[4] This is also marking a new phase of globalisation, which is seen as a post-globalisation or a second phase of globalisation. Whatever the label, it is argued that this new phase is bringing about the beginning of the end of the dominance of the 'Washington Consensus' (WC) and the neo-liberalism era. In this new period, the US will no longer own globalisation. It will no longer be the rule-maker and the rest of the world rule-takers. It seems that instead of convergence of forms of regulation, capitalism and routes to modernity, there will be increasing diversity under which 'each country plans to shape its own future its own way'.[5]

Furthermore, it may be right to argue that it is not globalisation but rather regionalisation that will become dominant in this new era because much of what has been regarded as globalisation was actually regionalisation.[6] As Hurrell has concluded 'the age of economic globalisation has also been the age of regionalisation'. With the latter becoming a major trend after the Cold War, and in the early years of the 21st century we 'have witnessed an intensification in regionalism across the globe'.[7] Some go further suggesting that 'the reality of the contemporary world seems to be better expressed in terms of regionalism'.[8] In economic terms, global power is concentrated in three regional groupings, known as the Triad, Europe (EU), East Asia (ASEAN Plus Three) and North America (NAFTA). These account for more than 75% of world merchandise trade, and nearly 70% of world GDP (see Table 2).

The increased regionalisation of the global system has been associated with the proliferation of formal regional arrangements. This has been termed 'new regionalism' and is characterised by regional blocs having a much stronger external orientation and playing a more important role in the global system by seeking to establish links with major powers as well as with each other. Thus, regional blocs have become major players in the global system and their interaction a new and

Table 2: The world's triad

	Population (2009)		GDP (2009)		Merchandise Trade (2007)	
	Million	%	$ billlion	%	$ billion	%
World	**6,438**	**100.0**	**68,651.5**	**100.0**	**28,194.0**	**100.0**
EU	497	7.7	14,774.0	21.6	10,894.0	38.6
NATFA	480	7.5	16,788.0	24.2	4,537.0	16.1
APT[1]	2,002	31.1	16,708.5	24.1	5,878.7	21.0
Total	**2,979**	**46.3**	**48,270.5**	**69.9**	**21,309.7**	**75.7**

Note: [1] ASEAN Plus Three (ASEAN + China, Japan and S.Korea)
Sources: *World Economic Outlook Database*, IMF 2009;
International Trade Statistic, WTO 2008

growing feature of international relations. The interaction between blocs, which have become increasingly governed by formal arrangements, has been termed 'interregionalism'.[9]

In the rise of interregionalism as a major feature of international relations, the EU has taken a lead. Indeed, the EU is regarded as 'the patron saint of interregionalism', and interregionalism has become a central and highly visible feature of the EU foreign policy.[10] The EU has now revived or/and established its relations with various regional groups, such as Southern Common Market (MERCOSUR), Southern African Development Community (SADC), Gulf Cooperation Council (GCC), South Asian Association for Regional Cooperation (SAARC). Rather less overtly ASEAN has also sought to develop this new form of international relations with almost all regional groupings.

2. New regionalism

2.1. Characteristics of new regionalism

Regionalism is not entirely new. It can be traced back to
the 19th century, when a number of trade agreements
were established in Europe, such as the customs unions
between the Austrian and Nordic states. This is
considered as the first of the four waves of regionalism
identified by Dicken.[11] The second wave of regionalism
took place after the World War I. The third one emerged
after the World War II and lasted until the 1970s. Finally,
the fourth and current one started during the late 1980s.
However, only the two last waves of regionalism, namely
the third and the fourth, have attracted much attention,
with the former named as old regionalism, and the latter
the labelled as 'new regionalism'.

The first key characteristic, which makes the current
regionalism *new*, is the sheer number of formal regional
arrangements. Between 1995 and 2000 an additional one
hundred regional trade agreements were established.[12]
As a result, many countries are members of at least one
regional organisation and some are members of more
than one (see Tables 3 and 4). Unlike the old regionalism,
which was a predominantly Eurocentric, the new is a
truly worldwide phenomenon, covering both more and
less developed countries, and in some cases, combining
both in the same regional organisation. In addition, while
the old regionalism had specific and narrowly defined
aims, either primarily security or economically oriented,
the new is a more comprehensive and multifaceted
process. It focuses not only on trade and security

Table 3: Name, membership, date(s) and type of main regional organisations

Name	Membership	Date(s)	Type
EU	Austria, Belgium, Bulgaria, Cyprus, Czech Republic, Denmark, Estonia, France, Finland, Germany, Greece, Hungary, Ireland, Italy, Latvia, Lithunia, Luxembourg, Malta, Netherlands, Poland, Portugal, Roumania, Slovakia, Slovenia, Spain, Sweeden, United Kingdom	1957 (EC) 1992 (EU)	Economic union
NAFTA	Canada, Mexico, United States	1994	FTA
MERCOSUR	Argentina, Brazil, Paraguay, Urguguay	1991	Common market
ANCOM	Bolivia, Colombia, Ecuardo, Peru, Venezuela	1969 Revised 1990	Customs union
CARICOM	Antigua & Barbuda, Bahamas, Barbados, Belize, Dominica, Grenada, Guyana, Haiti, Jamaica, Montserrat, St Kitts & Nevis, St Lucia, St Vincent & the Grenadines, Suriname, Trinidad & Tobago	1973	FTA
ASEAN	Brunei, Cambodia, Indonesia, Laos, Malaysia, Myanmar, Philippines, Singapore, Thailand and Vietnam	1967	FTA
SAARC	Bangladesh, Bhutan, India, Maldives, Nepal, Pakistan and Sri Lanka	1985	FTA
SADC	Angola, Botswana, Lesotho, Malawi, Mozambique, Swaziland, United Republic of Tanzania, Zambia and Zimbabwe	1980 Revised 1992	FTA
ECOWAS	Benin, Burkina Faso, Cabe Verde, Ivory Coast, Gambia, Ghana, Guinee, Guinee Bissau, Liberia, Mali, Niger, Nigeria, Senegal, Sierra Lenone, Togo	1975	Customs union
GCC	Bahrain, Kuwait, Oman, Qatar, Saudi Arabia, The United Arab Emirates	1981	Common market

Xuan Loc Doan

Table 4: Population, GDP and merchandise trade of major regional organisations

	Population (2009)		GDP (2009)		Merchandise Trade (2007)	
	Million	% World	$ Billion	% World	$ Billion	% World
World	**6,437**	**100.0**	**68,651.5**	**100.0**	**28,194.0**	**100.0**
EU	493	7.7	14,774.0	21.6	10,894.0	38.6
NAFTA	480	7.5	16,788.0	24.2	4,537.0	16.1
MERCOSUR	244	3.8	2,616.3	3.8	408.0	1.7
ANCOM	131	2.0	116.2	1.7	146.3	0.5
CARICOM	16	0.2	91.4	0.1	46.6	0.2
ASEAN	591	9.2	2,774.5	4.1	1,638.0	5.8
SARRC	1,584	24.6	4,295.5	6.1	468.7	1.7
SADC	111	1.7	243.8	0.4	280.1	1.0
ECOSWAS	291	4.5	507.7	0.7	145.0	0.5
GCC	38	0.6	1,125.6	1.7	845.4	3.0
Total	**3,979**	**61.8**	**43,333.0**	**64.4**	**19,409.1**	**69.1**

Sources: *World Economic Outlook Database*, IMF 2009; *International Trade Statistic*, WTO 2008

integration and cooperation but also on other areas, such as the environment, social policy or monetary cooperation and integration. As Farrell puts it, the new regionalism is 'a multidimensional form of integration embracing economic, cultural, political and social aspects, thereby extending the understanding of regional activities beyond the creation of free trade agreements or security'.[13] New regionalism also differs in terms of its impact. While the old regionalism, with the exception of the European Community, had a very modest success, the new has become a prominent force, 'shaping the politics of the contemporary world economy'.[14] Lastly and most importantly, while the old regionalism was formed and defined by the bipolar rivalry, the new is taking shape in an increasingly multipolar world. In other words, contrary to the earlier regionalism, which was mainly created from 'above', that is by the support or the intention of the superpowers, particularly of the US,[15] the latter is a more spontaneous development, which generates from 'below' and 'within' a particular region. That is why the old regionalism is known as the *hegemonic regionalism*, whereas the new is referred to as the *autonomous regionalism*.

It should be stressed that while new regionalism is a multifaceted phenomenon, covering virtually all spheres and areas, its major focus remains trade. However, the way these regional trade blocs are organised and the level to which they reach are very different from each other. Among the existing regional economic arrangements, four different types of regional economic integration can be identified. The first is the free trade area (FTA), in which trade restrictions between member states are removed but where member states retain their individual trade policies towards non-members. The majority of the existing regional arrangements are in this form, such as ASEAN Free Trade Agreement (AFTA), signed in 1992 and NAFTA, engaged in 1994. The next level is a customs union, in which, in addition to establishing a FTA with each other, member states have a common external trade policy (tariffs or non-tariff barriers) with outsiders. Andean Common Market (ANCOM), which was established in 1969 and revived in 1990s, is an example of this. The third form is a common market, in which not only are trade barriers between member states removed and a common external trade policy adopted but also the free movements of services, capital and labour between member states is permitted. MERCOSUR, which was established in 1991, and the ASEAN Economic Community (AEC), which is planned to be fully operational by 2015, are two examples of this. The last and highest form of regional economic cooperation is an economic union, in which, addition to the elements included in the three aforementioned forms, economic and monetary policies are set by and subject to supranational control. So far, there is only one group, which is so highly integrated to come close to being a true economic union, namely the EU (see Table 3).

2.2. Regionalism and globalisation

The above sections have singled out some key characteristics and forms of contemporary regionalism. However, the key issues are why regional blocs have been revived or formed, and to what extent they have impacted on the global system, in general, and on the multipolarity, in particular. First, with regard to the motives of the new regionalism, given their multifaceted nature it is not an easy task to single out the rationales behind regional projects. Nevertheless, according to Farrell, there are two key premises that most commentators see as critical. The first one, which takes an outside-in perspective by focussing on external/global pressures or challenges, argues that 'regionalism is a response to globalisation and a reaction to the diverse aspects of global processes in their entirety'. The second premise, which takes an inside-out perspective by emphasising internal/regional elements, 'is based upon the recognition that regionalism emerges from internal dynamics of the region, and the motivations and strategies of regional actors'.[16]

According to the first premise, there are close links between regionalism and globalisation because it is widely argued that globalisation has both positive and negative consequences for nation states, which respond by using regionalism as both a defensive and an offensive strategy. Hurrell maintains that the links between the two phenomena have been, and remain very important. According to him, 'regionalism is seen as a critical part of the political economy of globalisation and of the strategies that states have adopted in the face of globalisation'. He points out that for some regionalism is 'a conscious attempt to assert political control over increased economic liberalisation and globalisation'. For others it is employed either to reproduce dominant forms of neoliberal economic governance at the regional level, or to serve 'as a form of resistance to globalisation and as a platform where alternative norms and practices can be developed'.[17]

From what has been said, there are two key (and contrasting) tendencies in the relationship between globalisation and regionalism. On one hand, regionalism goes with globalisation, by helping participating countries to enter and engage with, or to have a more influential role in the global economy. On the other hand, it is used to provide an alternative and/or resistance to globalisation. With regard to the former, it can be said that for participating countries, especially weaker or developing countries, regionalism is a way for them to enter and remain engaged with the global economy. That is regionalism enable them to enter the Western-dominated order, in which their interests are often perceived as marginalised. In her study of the regionalism in the Asia-Pacific region, Nesadurai argues that Asian countries pursue regionalism in order to counter just such marginalisation within the global economy.[18] Similarly, it is also believed that, without joining NAFTA, 'Canada and Mexico had limited options by going it alone in a global economy'.[19] For stronger and more developed countries, regionalism provides a further influence in the global economy. One of the key factors that pushed the US to establish NAFTA was to search for further advantage in a world, which is increasingly regionalised. China actively participates in regional projects in East Asia, not only because it wishes to engage in the global economy, but also to attempt to enhance its international influence. From this point of view, countries, especially developing and weaker ones, adopt neoliberal norms and practices to engage with the global economy. This neoliberal approach is also known as the Washington Consensus (WC), which advocated for economic liberalisation, deregulation and privatisation and the creation of a single global market.

However, liberalisation as advocated by the WC has been increasingly challenged by those who criticised and opposed the market fundamentalism of globalisation project. More importantly, as the 1997-1998 Asian financial crises, which also spread to Latin America, showed, the neoliberal norms and practices have brought about great risks. These crises were seen as a setback to the advance of Western style capitalism. That is why the emerging markets, especially those from Asia and Latin America, increasingly tend to shift the focus from the WC 'towards a post-Washington Consensus (PWC), which includes the global agenda of mechanisms to mitigate the backlash against global liberalization'.[20] In this context, it can be argued that regionalism can provide an effective means to legitimate or regulate globalisation by mitigating its worst excesses.

According to the second premise, the regional projects of the new regionalism are formed from 'below' and 'within' a particular region. Because of this the current wave of regionalism 'is really made up of many different regionalisms, reflecting different conditions, values and even ideological positions across the global arena – it is a product of the historical, social and political conditions of specific regions'.[21] In other words, regional groupings are formed to meet the specific challenges/demands of their particular member countries as well as their regions. For instance, for Southeast Asian countries, regional projects such as the ASEAN Regional Forum (ARF) or the ASEAN Plus Three (APT) were established in order to meet regional countries' concerns over regional security, and the containment of China. MERCOSUR was designed to bring Brazil and Argentina closer together, as was the case of France and West Germany at the beginning of the European construction.

In sum, distinct patterns and forms of regional projects have emerged and continue to develop their own particular rhythm around the world. They have been formed by the regional/internal dynamics of particular regions on the one hand, and by external pressure such as globalisation on the other. So regionalism is seen as both a defensive and an offensive strategy that the participating countries use to respond to the positive and negative aspects of globalisation. It is also used to meet the particular concerns or challenges of the particular countries of a specific region.

2.3. Regionalism and world order

Regionalism is also seen as one of the contending world order projects. As has already been underlined, contemporary regionalism has become a major force shaping the world. This is because it has brought about the proliferation of regional blocs/actors, which have increasingly played influential roles in the global system. According to Padoan, there are two main features that are likely to characterise the evolution of the international system in the foreseeable future.[22] One is the emergence of new world leaders such as China and India, which strengthens the trend towards a multipolar system. The other is the emergence of regional agreements/blocs, 'a club of clubs', which are expected to exist alongside single major powers and pursue independent and, possibly conflicting, policies vis-à-vis the latter. As is developed in more detail below, one of the key factors that pushed ASEAN states to establish the ASEAN free trade area, and more recently an ASEAN Economic Community, was the need to increase their bargaining power vis-à-vis regional major powers, India, Japan and particularly China. All of these have also become actively engaged in regional projects, such as APT and the East Asian Summit. In his study of China's attitude towards regionalism, Zhang concluded that China's leaders have reconstructed the country's self-identity in a dualist form: a developing country in the era of globalisation, on one hand, and a potential responsible world power in the international system, on the other.[23] This is because Chinese elites perceive the emergence of a multipolar world in which China will be one of the major poles. One of the key ways for China to become a responsible global player in this multipolar world is to participate in regional and transregional economic and security schemes. In short, there is no doubt that regionalism and regional blocs are coming to play a role in the world order in general, and multipolarity, in particular. The questions are in what manner and to what extent.

Before exploring these questions, it is helpful to define the world order. Hettne opts for a non-normative approach, depicting the world order, comprising three dimensions: structure, mode of governance, and form of legitimacy. Concerning the structural dimension, which is about the way the units of the system are related, a distinction is made between unipolar, bipolar and multipolar. With regard to the mode of governance, which refers to avenues of influence on decision-making and policy-making, three modes of governance are distinguished namely unilateral, plurilateral and multilateral. Legitimacy is the basis on which the system is made acceptable to the constituent units. Going back to the question asked earlier, Hettne points out that whether the regional organisations play an important role in the world order depends on which form of the world order one envisages. One possible form could be a neo-Westphalian order, governed either by a reconstructed UN system, in which the world's major regions have a strong influence or by a more loosely organised global concert of great powers and the consequent marginalisation of the UN. In the former case, both the role of the UN and the world's major regions are emphasised. This world order, which is supported by the EU, is 'preferable in terms of legitimacy, but as several unsuccessful attempts proved, hard to achieve'. In the latter case, 'regionalism will suffer from imposed or hegemonic regionalism'.[24] This world order, which is supported by the US, 'is more realistic but dangerously similar to the old balance-of-power politics'.[25] However, according to Hettne, regionalism can put its mark on a future world order by creating a third possibility, namely a 'post-Westphalian' order, in which 'the locus of power would move irreversibly to the transnational level; and the state system would be replaced or complemented by a regionalised world order', which is strongly preferred by the EU.[26]

Which of these three forms of the world order will emerge depends not only on the attitude of the US and major powers but also on the willingness and capacity of regional blocs/actors to strengthen their own regional groupings. The next sections, which examine the major regional groupings, will provide a better understanding of the impact of regional groupings on the world order in general, and on multipolarity, in particular. The study of different regional groupings also enables us to understand more fully the motives of regionalism.

2.4. Some major regional organisations
The European Union
The EU is now the most economically, politically and institutionally integrated of all the world's regional organisations. It is also the most powerful and complex institution. While it is beyond the scope of this study to review the whole process of EU development and integration, there are some key issues that should be underlined. First, even though the primary objective of European integration was to prevent conflict between the European states, notably between Germany and France, from the outset European integration had a strong economic rationale. Indeed, from the beginning it went beyond the idea of a free trade area with the key objective of the Treaty of Rome being the establishment a common market. Thus, in economic terms, 'the European integration has fed on, and contributed to, the global trend towards neoliberal economic policy, with its emphasis on liberal trade'.[27] Indeed, the underlying objective of the EU has been market liberalisation, which has been more effective and more far-reaching than elsewhere in the world. In addition, the EU has a single currency and common policies areas, such as citizenship. Thus, European integration can be seen as 'turbo-charged globalisation', as 'a regional expression of globalisation, accelerating the transnational nature of

markets and thus further disenfranchising states and society'.[28] However, European integration is also perceived as a response to, or a protection against the negative aspects of globalisation. In other words, the EU is considered as a mechanism through which states and society not only regain a degree of control over markets but also are able to deal effectively with a number of transnational issues such as the environment, health, migration or crime. In this sense, the European model is very different from, if not in opposition to, the US's *laissez faire* capitalism. According to Kupchan 'the two sides of the Atlantic are drifting apart because they follow two different social models'.[29]

The second point is the recognition that the EU has become a global actor on the international stage.[30] In economic terms, the EU is undoubtedly a formidable power. It comprises 27 countries, with a population of nearly 500 million, accounting for 21.6% of world GDP, and 38.6% of world merchandise trade (see Table 4). In addition, the EU has a 'comprehensive array of legal, diplomatic and military (to a certain degree) means, and notably the Euro – the world's second most important international reserve and trade currency, which unquestionably enable it to exercise significant influence in various part of the world'.[31] It has become a major force in international affairs, especially in trade, development cooperation, climate change, the promotion of regional integration and to an increasing extent, in security issues. Moreover, the EU not only speaks with a single voice and acts as a single actor on many issues, but also has developed its own approach to international affairs. This has brought it to directly oppose some of the policies of the US. The opposition to the Iraq War of France, Germany and some other EU members, described by the US's former Defense Secretary Donald Rumsfeld as the 'Old Europe', is an example of this. Even though not all EU members opposed this war (indeed, the members of the so-called 'New Europe' supported it), the disputes between France, Germany, two the US's main European allies, and the US, demonstrated the divergences between the EU and the US. Kagan, in his famous and controversial study of the transatlantic relations, argues that there is a growing divergence between Europe and the US because they have different views of the world. According to him, while the former stresses 'soft power', such as international laws and cooperation, as the efficient way to advance peace in the world, the latter promotes a global order and stability through the possession and use of military power.[32] In sum, the EU has a clear and distinct approach to shape the world order, which emphasises dialogue, international law, institutionalised relations, and multilateralism. Thus, the EU has been increasingly referred to as a 'civilian power' or 'a normative power'.[33]

However, the most significant characteristics of the EU external relations, which is also the third point that should be underlined here, is that the EU has strongly fostered its links with other regional organisations/groupings (Table 5). The EU is the hub of interregional arrangements, encompassing not only trade and foreign investment but also political dialogue and cultural relations.

To conclude, first, it is right to argue that the EU is a major power in the global system. In economic terms, it

Table 5: EU's trade with main regional organisations and countries

	Import		Export		Import + Export	
	Billion €	%	Billion €	%	Million €	%
World	**1,426.0**	**100.0**	**1,240.0**	**100.0**	**2,666.0**	**100.0**
NAFTA	216.3	15.2	308.2	24.9	524.6	19.7
ASEAN	80.3	5.6	54.5	4.4	135.0	5.1
GCC	30.6	2.2	61.5	5.0	92.2	3.3
Total	**327.2**	**23.0**	**424.4**	**34.3**	**752.0**	**28.1**
China	231.5	16.2	72.0	5.8	303.3	11.4
Russia	144.0	10.1	89.1	7.2	233.0	8.7
Switzerland	76.7	5.4	93.0	7.5	169.5	6.4
Total	**452.2**	**31.7**	**254.1**	**20.5**	**705.8**	**26.5**

Source: *EUROSTAT*, DG Trade 2008

is one of the three pillars, if not the strongest one, in the world economy. Second, thanks to its economic power, the EU has increasingly become a global actor and developed its own approach to the global affairs. A notable feature of this European approach is its preference for interregionalism. In other words, it seems that the EU seeks to build a world order, which is multipolar and multilateral, in which regional organisations/blocs and their links with each other play an important role. However, whether this world order can be feasible and realistic or not depends on many factors. One is whether the US is willing to shift its foreign policy form unilateralism towards multilateralism. Moreover, it depends on whether the EU and other regional actors are able to develop and strengthen their *actorness*, that is their capacity to act in the global system, or whether they can find the common approach to common issues they face. We will go back to these points later in the section on interregionalism.

The Asia-Pacific

The starting point for any discussion of regional cooperation in the Asia-Pacific region must be the Association of Southeast Asian Nations (ASEAN) (see Table 6). This is one of the most lasting and significant regional organisations outside Europe. In addition, ASEAN states are involved in all the regional projects or mechanisms in East Asia and Asia-Pacific, either initiating them or shaping the form taken by them. ASEAN was formed in 1967, when the foreign ministers of the five founding members, Indonesia, Malaysia, Philippines, Singapore and Thailand, signed the Bangkok Declaration. It now encompasses all ten Southeast Asian nations, after the adherence of Brunei in 1994, Vietnam in 1995, Laos and Myanmar in 1997 and Cambodia in 1999. Born at the height of the Cold War, ASEAN's basic underpinnings were primarily political-security concerns, even though its founding document only mentioned economic, social and cultural cooperation. However, ASEAN's leaders did not begin to think seriously about economic cooperation until the early 1990s. The ASEAN Free Trade Area (AFTA) was proposed in 1991 and was signed at its Singapore Summit in 1992. It was ASEAN's response to the implications of the Uruguay Round, namely that global trade liberalisation was inevitable. Moreover, there was a realisation that ASEAN needed to reinvent itself in

Table 6: ASEAN's trade with main regional organisations and countries

	Import		Export		Import + Export	
	Billion €	%	Billion €	%	Billion €	%
World	**561.2**	**100.0**	**629.0**	**100.0**	**1,190.0**	**100.0**
EU	60.3	10.7	80.1	12.7	140.4	11.8
NAFTA	58.0	10.3	88.0	14.0	146.0	12.3
GCC	37.0	6.6	13.5	2.1	50.4	4.2
Total	**155.3**	**27.6**	**181.6**	**28.9**	**336.8**	**28.3**
China	76.2	13.6	68.2	10.9	144.5	12.1
Japan	70.4	12.5	65.0	10.3	135.1	11.4
Korea	30.0	5.3	24.2	3.9	54.1	4.6
Total	**176.6**	**31.3**	**157.4**	**25.1**	**333.7**	**28.1**

Source: *EUROSTAT*, DG Trade 2008

order to adapt to the new geopolitical environment brought about by the end of the Cold War.

In addition to the establishment of the AFTA, ASEAN states participate in the Asia-Pacific Economic Cooperation (APEC). This forum, which was established in 1989, is not regional but transregional, with a membership that includes not only East and Southeast Asian countries, but also Australia, New Zealand, Canada, Mexico, Chile and the US. Initially, Southeast Asian countries were reserved about this forum because they feared that the US would dominate it. However, eventually they actively engaged, partly because of the fear of being marginalised in the all-important US market, and partly because they hoped to engage the US in the region. Despite its shift to economic issues, security remains a primary concern for ASEAN states. In the aftermath of the Cold War the rise of China led to power shifts and uncertainties in the region. This prompted ASEAN states to form the ASEAN Regional Forum (ARF) in 1994 to deal with regional security issues.[34] Like APEC, ARF is not a regional organisation but a trans-regional forum with members from three different regions/continents, North America (US), Europe (EU and Russia) and Asia. Because it involves all the regional and world powers, the ARF can be seen as the United Nations for/in Asia. In both arrangements, ASEAN remains the core and their *modus operandi* is the 'ASEAN way'. While the ARF is seen as an extension of ASEAN, APEC not only adheres to the 'ASEAN way' of working but its 'summits are always held in a strict two-year rotation of an ASEAN country and a non-ASEAN country'.[35] Another significant institution that ASEAN states initiated and that will be discussed more in detail later is the Asia-Europe Meeting (ASEM), which was established in 1996.

The 1997-1998 financial crisis and ASEAN's failure to respond to this, and other regional challenges, such as the Myanmar issue, damaged ASEAN's relevance and credibility. This has led to attempts to increase regional cohesion and integration, and raise the region's bargaining power with extra-regional players. One of these efforts was the agreement to establish by 2020 an ASEAN Economic Community (AEC), to facilitate the free flow of goods, services, and capital. The latest and most significant attempt is ASEAN's agreement to sign the ASEAN Charter at the Singapore Summit in 2007. After 40 years of existence, ASEAN was given a legal and institutional framework, which included an ASEAN Human Rights Body to deal with this sensitive issue. In addition, the ASEAN states have sought to engage with their major Asian neighbours, South Korea, Japan and, in particular, China. These have contributed to the creation of a new type of regionalism in East Asia, known as ASEAN Plus Three (APT; see Table 2). This new mechanism was established because Asian observers increasingly evaluated APEC as a tool of the US's policy. Moreover, it was perceived as ASEAN's response to APEC's failure in general, and the US's reluctance, in particular, to help Southeast Asia during the 1997-1998 crisis. In an effort to help the regional states to cope with any similar future crisis, at the 2000 Chiang Mai Summit, the leaders of the APT launched an initiative, known as the Chiang Mai Initiative (CMI), which was 'a currency swap arrangement between central banks enabling member states to protect against future speculative attacks on their currency'.[36] More recently and significantly, in an effort to overcome the global financial crisis, in May 2009, the ATP countries took a much more robust step by creating a US $120 billion foreign-exchange reserves pool. This fund is not only the region's concerted effort to recover from the crisis but also illustrates the region's desire and attempt to be self-reliant in crisis. Another significant development in the region, which was designed to foster a wider Asian regionalism, was the inauguration of the East Asian Summit (EAS) in December 2005. This includes the members of ATP together with India, Australia and New Zealand. For optimistic observers, the EAS can be seen as the first step towards creating an East Asia Community (EAC) like the European Community or a free trade area like NAFTA.[37]

All the above regional projects have included the East Asian states, and some of South Asia, as well as ASEAN. These countries have participated either to avoid marginalisation or to seek domination. China has actively participated in regional and transregional economic and security schemes as part of its desire for modernisation as well as to enhance its international influence and to promote its relations with ASEAN and other Asian countries. Similarly, India has also sought to develop links with ASEAN and wishes to be involved in the EAS.[38]

There are some clear conclusions. First, prior to the 1997-1998 financial crisis, the neoliberal economic agenda, that is trade and investment liberalisation, dominated the regional and transregional projects, namely the AFTA and APEC. Participants, especially those in Southeast Asian, initiated and became involved in these mechanisms because of concerns over their potential marginalisation in the world economy. In this sense, economic regionalism was seen as a way for them to engage more fully in the global economy. However, in the post-crisis period, even though still keeping the neoliberal approach to global engagement Asian countries initiated mechanisms to regulate globalisation or to mitigate its negative consequences.[39] The CMI or the recent US$ 120 billion regional fund is an example of this. Moreover, the key characteristic of the Asian regionalism, as the APT, EAS, EAC, or the CMI demonstrate, in the post-crisis period, is the intentional exclusion of the US.[40] This is a notable development, given the important role of the US in the region. It is worth noting that the idea of an exclusive Asian regionalism, namely the East Asian Economic Caucus (EAEC), had been championed by former Malaysian Prime Minister Mahathir Mohamad since early 1990s. However, due to the US's opposition and rejection by Japan, the US's ally, it did not materialise. Now, it seems that the US is unlikely able to block these developments as easily as it did during 1990s.[41] Furthermore, the recent agreement of the APT to establish the regional emergency fund, which can eventually lead to the creation of an Asian Monetary Fund (AMF), is strong evidence that the region's countries want to cut their dependence on the West and the Bretton Woods institutions. Again, the proposal to create the AMF was put forwards at the outbreak of the Asian financial crisis a decade ago. However, due to the US's opposition it was withdrawn. Yet, now the US cannot stop the region's countries from doing so.

It is perhaps still too early and too optimistic to think that the Chiang Mai Initiative or the regional fund will lead to financial integration in the region or that the East Asian Community will be established in the near future. Indeed, for pessimists, given the asymmetry of economic development levels, the divergences of geopolitical interests, strategic rivalries, deep-seated distrust, for the moment the establishment such a community seems impossible.[42] Yet, the very fact that ASEAN members and other East Asian countries are thinking about and discussing such a development implies that they believe that a formal East Asian region is both necessary and possible in the 21st century. If it is realised it will be a development of long-term global significance. In economic terms, in addition to ASEAN states, this region involves three of the world's economic powerhouses, (Japan and two emerging powers, namely China and India). The trade within ASEAN accounts for only 25% of total ASEAN trade, which is much smaller than that of NAFTA and the EU, which respectively accounts for 51% and 68% of their total trade. However, the trade within the Asia-Pacific region (ASEAN and East Asian) accounts for 50% of their total trade, approximately similar to that of NAFTA. This intensification of intra-regional trade or regionalisation is likely to further the formal processes of regionalism.

The Americas

As in Western Europe and Southeast Asia, regionalism is not new in the Americas. Various regional arrangements were established in Latin America and the Caribbean region during the 1960s and 1970s, such as the Central American Common Market (CACM), established in 1960, the Latin American Free Trade Association (LAFTA) in 1960, the Andean Community (or ANCOM) in 1969, and the Caribbean Community (CARICOM) in 1973. However, like regional integration worldwide, regionalism in the Americas became much more important during the 1990s when many regional projects were revived and new ones initiated. The most important, at least in terms of its economic weight and

Table 7: NAFTA's trade with main regional organisations and countries

	Import		Export		Import + Export	
	Million €	%	Million €	%	Million €	%
World	**1,938.2**	**100.0**	**1,318.3**	**100.0**	**3,256.5**	**100.0**
EU	326.0	16.8	232.0	16.2	539.5	16.6
ASEAN	96.0	5.0	48.0	3.6	143.6	4.4
GCC	31.5	1.6	25.2	1.9	57.0	1.7
Total	**453.5**	**23.4**	**305.2**	**21.7**	**740.0**	**22.7**
China	288.0	14.8	56.0	4.3	343.6	10.6
Japan	128.5	6.6	54.0	4.1	183.0	5.6
Korea	51.0	2.6	28.0	2.1	78.4	2.4
Total	**447.5**	**24.0**	**138.0**	**10.5**	**605.0**	**18.6**

Source: *EUROSTAT*, DG Trade 2008

wider impact, are North American Free Trade Area (NAFTA), in the North, and MERCOSUR in the South.

NAFTA, which came into force 1994, includes the US, Canada and Mexico (see Table 7). However, the deciding actor in the foundation, development and the success (or failure) of this regional project was (and continues to be) the US. NAFTA was seen, first and foremost, as the US's response to the revival of the European integration, that is the Single European Act, which the US believed could lead to the 'European Fortress'. The US's establishment of the FTA with its wealthy northern neighbour in 1989 and with its much poorer southern neighbour in 1994 marked a new chapter in the US's foreign trade policy. Hitherto, the US had approached the liberalisation of international trade through multilateralism, that is through GATT. Sbragia sees this shift to regionalism as having two causes. First, the end of the Cold War made the multilateral arrangements that the US favoured less relevant. Second, the very success of the European integration 'led the US to change its international economic policy so as to embrace a preferential trading area into its portfolio'.[43] In sum, for the US, NAFTA, besides allowing it to have access to Mexican raw materials, markets and low labour costs, could give it further leverage in a world which is increasingly regionalised. Similarly, Canada and Mexico would find it much easier to increase their engagement with the global economies as members of a regional body. For Mexico, the FTA could help to attract foreign investment, not only from the US but also from Europe and Asia, and secure access to the huge markets of the US and Canada.

After fifteen years of existence, there are still very mixed views about NAFTA. For its critics, there is no cause for celebration and 'the trade pact must be fixed or ditched'.[44] During the 2008 presidential campaign, both Democrat candidates, Hillary Clinton and Barack Obama repeated their pledge that if elected they would renegotiate NAFTA or opt out because of their concerns about, environmental and labour impacts.[45] In Mexico, there were fears that the country was becoming even more dominated by the US. However, according to Hufbauer and Schott most economists believe that NAFTA is a tremendous success, bringing about better jobs and higher incomes to the three members.[46] Since NAFTA came into force, trade between three members has increased more than threefold. According to recent polls, 72% of Canadians and 62% of Mexicans support NAFTA. In the US, the support is much lower, with 49%

believing the NAFTA is good for the US while 39% say it is bad.[47]

On the international front, it is believed that American regionalism, in general, and NAFTA in particular, gives the US a powerful bargaining chip in multilateral negotiations, enabling the forcing of concessions from the EU in bilateral and global negotiations.[48] Yet, despite having reached its 15th anniversary (January 2009), NAFTA remains a free trade area; it is unlikely to develop into an economic union, such as the EU, or a common market like MERCOSUR, unless there is a major shift in economic and political developments globally, and more particularly, in the US's domestic politics.[49]

In South America, the most important grouping is MERCOSUR, which was established by Argentina, Brazil, Paraguay and Uruguay in 1991. The Treaty of Asunción, the founding treaty, set out a three-stage programme. A free trade area was to be created by 1994, succeeded in 1995 by a customs union, which would lead to the establishment of a common market and a common external commercial policy. The rationale behind the establishment of MERCOSUR was political. As was the case with France and West Germany at the beginning of the European construction, the regional agreement was designed to bring Brazil and Argentina closer together. Moreover, as these two countries were in a transitionary period, moving from the dictatorship to constitutional democracy, MERCOSUR was aimed at strengthening democracy. However, as is clearly documented in the founding treaty, the economic aspect also played a crucial role in the foundation of MERCOSUR. As Mecham notes, a challenge for South America, as for other developing regions, was how to integrate into the global economy.[50] The response to this challenge was to embrace regionalism and the neoliberal economic model outlined by the Washington Consensus. Thus, MERCOSUR was predicated on liberalisation and commercial openness, both among the member states and towards the outside world. Another important factor leading to the creation of MERCOSUR was the concern of members, particularly Brazil, with the hegemonic power of the US.[51] Just as NAFTA is dominated and institutionalised for foreign economy policy purposes by the US, so Brazil not only dominates MERCOSUR but also sees it as a vehicle to strengthen its regional power base.[52]

MERCOSUR initially enjoyed great success with trade among its member increased fivefold, from US$ 8 billion in 1990 to US$ 41 billion in 1998. During the same period, there was also a rise in the share of MERCOSUR's total world trade from 11% to 23%.[53] However, as in Southeast Asia, the financial crisis of the late 1990s greatly weakened MERCOSUR. Among its four members, Argentina suffered the most, being 'plunged into an economic crisis lasting four years, mainly as a result of 1999 Brazilian currency devaluation', and verged on economic collapse.[54] Coming out of the crisis in a much weaker position than Brazil, Argentina started to question the *raison d'être* of MERCOSUR and wished to become closer to the US in order to foster a Free Trade Area of the Americas (FTAA), a wider regional project initiated by the US. Brazil, under the Lula da Silva administration, on one hand, began to have second thought about MERCOSUR as it focused on internal issues, such as the social agenda and the fight against the poverty. On the other, it shifted its regional and international priorities towards the building of a broader South American Community as a response the US's FTAA. Given these different priorities of its two key members, MERCOSUR integration was undermined.

In addition to the aforementioned regional arrangements, the US and Brazil proposed broader and different or even opposing regional mechanisms. With regard to the US, since the early 1990s, President Bill Clinton launched the negotiation to create a pan-hemispheric FTA, encompassing all 34 countries from North, Central and South America, that would achieve economic integration through trade and investment. As a first stage, the US sought bilateral agreements with individual South American countries. The purpose of this tactic was 'to strengthen a US-friendly NAFTA model over the more developmentalist version preferred by Brazil and some other Latin American countries'.[55] However, even though several ministerial meetings and working groups were held to discuss issues such as market access, investments, services, and dispute settlements, no progress has been made in establishing the FTAA. One of the main reasons for this failure is that both the US and Brazil compete for economic and geopolitical influence in Latin America. Concerning Brazil, being concerned over the US hegemony in the region, it is attempting to create a South American Free Trade Area (SAFTA) by integrating two sub-regional associations, namely MERCOSUR and ANCOM. The

SAFTA was proposed by former Brazilian President Fernando Henrique Cardoso at a Summit of the presidents of MERCOSUR and ANCOM in Brasilia in 2000, and this is now becoming a core objective of the Lula da Silva administration. In 2002, MERCOSUR and ANCOM agreed in principle to establish SAFTA, and a year later, a Free Trade Agreement between the two blocs was signed. In 2004, they agreed to set up a South American Community of Nations (SACN). The declared objectives of this were the promotion of socio-economic development in Latin America. Yet, it is also seen as a response to the US attempts to create the FTAA. So far, the establishing the pan-American free trade area, advocated by the US, seems to be stalled, while the future of SAFTA and SACN initiated by Brazil, remain open issues. It is argued that by giving priority to the South American project, Brazil may risk weakening MERCOSUR, even though the Lula da Silva government maintains that there is no contradiction between the project of a South American Community of Nations and the deepening of MERCOSUR.

Africa and others

As elsewhere, regionalism is not completely new in Africa. The Southern African Customs Union came into existence in December 1969 and the list of both past and present multilateral economic agreements is probably longer than that relating to any other continent. The Economic Community of West African States (ECOWAS), founded in 1975, the Southern African Development Coordination Conference (SADCC), established in 1980s and later in 1992, becoming the Southern African Development Community (SADC), are only two among these (see Tables 3 and 4). According to Telò, these regional projects were established for two main reasons. The first was the fear of being marginalised in the new international environment, characterised by globalisation and regionalisation; and the second was the external pressure by the international community, particularly through EU development policy.[56] However, in terms of its achievements, regionalism in Africa is very poor. Almost all regional trade initiatives in Africa 'have achieved very little in spite of their political appeal'.[57]

There are other regional arrangements around the world, such as the South Asian Association for Regional Cooperation (SAARC), which was established by India, Pakistan, Bangladesh, Sri Lanka, Nepal, Maldives and Bhutan in 1985 (see Tables 3 and 4). In the Arab world, there is the Arab Maghreb Union, which was established in 1987 by five Maghreb states, namely Algeria, Libya, Mauritania, Morocco, and Tunisia, and the Gulf Cooperation Council (GCC), which was formed in 1981. The GCC, which composes the six oil and gas producing states of the Persian Gulf, Bahrain, Kuwait, Oman, Qatar, Saudi Arabia and the United Arab Emirates, has achieved relatively important successes (see Table 8). As Baabood points out, a free trade area has been created and an agreement on a customs union entered into force in 2003.[58] There is already free movement of people, goods and capital between its member states. Furthermore, a monetary union with a single currency and a common Gulf citizenship have been under

Table 8: GCC's trade with main regional organisations and countries

	Import		Export		Import + Export	
	Billion €	%	Billion €	%	Billion €	%
World	**219.0**	**100.0**	**319.0**	**100.0**	**537.2**	**100.0**
EU	67.2	30.7	28.2	8.8	95.4	17.7
NAFTA	25.2	11.5	31.5	9.9	57.0	10.6
ASEAN	13.4	6.2	37.0	11.6	50.4	9.4
Total	**106.8**	**48.4**	**96.7**	**30.3**	**202.8**	**37.7**
China	22.0	10.1	20.0	6.3	42.1	7.8
Japan	17.3	7.9	66.0	20.7	83.2	15.5
Korea	6.5	3.0	35.0	10.9	41.2	7.7
Total	**45.8**	**21.0**	**121.0**	**37.9**	**166.5**	**31.0**

Source: *EUROSTAT*, DG Trade 2008

discussions. Overall, as it has been mentioned, these regional arrangements, except the GCC, are either unsuccessful or of little significance.

3. Interregionalism

3.1. Characteristics and forms of interregionalism

Interregionalism is not entirely new. It can be traced back to early 1960s when the European Community (EC) and the Associated African States established links in 1963. The EC subsequently established links with other regional groupings during the 1970s and early 1980s. However, until the end of the Cold War, the existence and importance of this form of interregionalism, known as region-to-region dialogues, went almost unnoticed (see Figure 1). This interregional network, which was often

Figure 1. Pre-1990 network of interregional dialogues

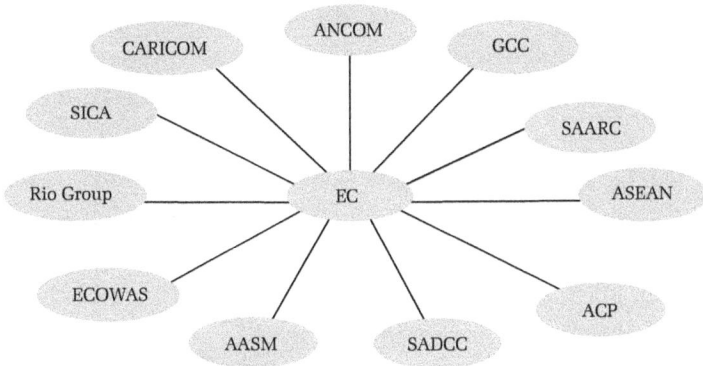

AASM:	Associated African States and Madagascar
ACP:	African, Caribbean and Pacific Group of States
ASEAN:	Association of Southeast Asian Nations
CARICOM:	Caribbean Community
EC:	European Community
ECOWAS:	Economic Community of West Afrian States
GCC:	Gulf Cooperation Council
SAARC:	South Asian Association for Regional Cooperation
SADCC:	Southern African Development Cooperation Conference
SICA:	Central American Integration System

referred to as a 'hub-and-spokes system', was developed within the narrow framework of bipolarity, which tended to overshadow it. This 'old interregionalism' like 'old regionalism' differed significantly from that which has developed since the early 1990s. Firstly, as with new regionalism, new interregionalism is taking shape in a post-Cold War world order. Secondly, unlike old interregionalism, which was primarily security and/or economically motivated, the new one is a more comprehensive and multidimensional phenomenon, covering different policy areas such as security, trade, finance, environment, migration and human rights. Thirdly, new interregionalism is closely connected, if not causally, to global structural transformations brought about by the end of the Cold War and globalisation. Last but not least, the new interregional projects are increasing rapidly in both number and variety (see Figure 2).

According to Hänggi, there are three types of external relations that regional organisations are developing, which are accordingly considered as three different forms of interregional arrangements.[59] The first form, and which is seen as *the* model of interregionalism, is the relationship between regional groupings, i.e. traditional region-to-region dialogues. Regional organisations involved in this form of interregionalism are institutionalised. Because of this, this type is often categorised as 'bilateral interregionalism' or 'pure interregionalism'. The region-to-region dialogues that the EU established with other regional groupings such as ASEAN or MERCOSUR are good examples of this. The second form, which is still terminologically disputed by scholars, can be described as a 'biregional' and 'transregional' relationship. This form, which is a rather recent phenomenon, is less institutionalised and its membership is more diffused. While in the biregional relationship its members are normally from two regions/continents, in the transregional form, members

Figure 2. Post-1990 network of interregional dialogues

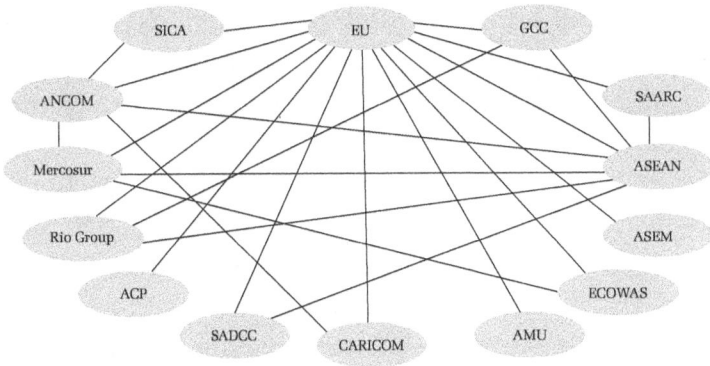

ACP:	African, Caribbean and Pacific Group of States
AMU:	Arab Maghreb Union
ASEAN:	Association of Southeast Asian Nations
ASEM:	Asia Europe Meeting
CARICOM:	Caribbean Community
ECOWAS:	Economic Community of West Afrian States
EU:	European Union
GCC:	Gulf Cooperation Council
SAARC:	South Asian Association for Regional Cooperation
SADCC:	Southern African Development Cooperation Conference
SICA:	Central American Integration System

belong to more than two regions/continents. The Asia-Europe Meeting (ASEM), the Europe-Latin America Summit launched in 1999 and the Europe-Africa Summit (2000) are the examples of biregional arrangements. The Asia Pacific Economic Cooperation (APEC), launched in 1989, or the ASEAN Regional

Forum (ARF), launched in 1994, are examples of transregional arrangements. The third 'form', which has also become quite prominent in recent years, is the relationships between regional groupings and single major powers, such as the EU's relationship with China, the US or Japan, or ASEAN's linkages with these major powers. If interregionalism is defined as the process of interaction between two regions, this third form can hardly considered as a form of interregionalism because it is not a relationship between two regions. However, if one takes the external relations of regional organisations as a point of departure in investigating interregional arrangements, then relationships between regional organisations and single major powers can be classed as a 'form' of interregionalism.

3.2. Nature and functions of interregionalism and regional actorness

The key question is why regional groupings and their respective members seek to forge interregional relationships. In exploring this, Rüland theorises the functions that interregionalism performs. The first function of interregionalism is *balancing*, which used to be mainly understood in military terms but is now increasingly measured in economic terms. In this sense and in this context, interregionalism is seen as an instrument by which regional groupings maintain or create a balance among themselves or against major powers. The second function is *institution-building*. This function, which is deduced from liberal institutionalism, means that when regional groupings establish interregional arrangements with one another they also strengthen the institutional coherence of the regional organisations involved. The third and fourth functions are *rationalising* and *agenda-setting*. It is argued that global multilateral forums have to deal with an increasingly complex issue and a growing number of actors, often representing extremely diverse interests'. Thus, these two functions of interregionalism can provide suitable means and platforms for improving the functioning of these global multilateral forums. The final function of inter- and transregional forums is *identity-building*. This function, which is theoretically deduced from constructivism, means that the interregional interaction may prompt the formation of collective identities.[60]

While Rüland uses a number of different theoretical perspectives to theorise the functions, Roloff combines neorealist and political-economy perspectives arguing that there are only two key main reasons, or in his words, two logics behind interregionalism, namely 'logic of complex of interdependence' and 'the logic of balance of power'. In other words, he believe that states seek to establish interregional relationships in order to manage the complex interdependence brought about by globalisation and pursue some kind of balance, that is 'a cooperative competition' between them.[61] Other scholars use a specific theoretical angle to approach a particular interregional relationship. Kupchan, who views the transatlantic interregionalism through realism, argues that interregionalism is a form of rival regionalism and the balancing games of different regional actors.[62] Investigating the operation of the Asia-Europe Meeting

(ASEM), Dent, from the perspective of liberalism, argues that regional actors cooperate with one another in order to manage complex interdependence,[63] while Gilson opting for a constructivist approach, maintained that its main objective is regional identity-building.[64] Holland, who studied Europe's engagement with African, Caribbean and Pacific groupings, also highlights the importance of regional identity-building.[65]

In their study of the role of interregionalism in EU foreign policy and external relations, Söderbaum *et al.* point out that there are three main factors behind the EU interregionalism: promoting liberal internationalism, building the EU as a global actor, and promoting EU power and competitiveness. Among these three, the two last objectives are related, or similar, to the functions of identity-building and balancing.[66] That is, by varying and strengthening their external relations, the EU seeks to develop and consolidate its own identity and presence as a global actor. The European Commission's Communication on the EU's relations with Asia states: 'There is one clear core objective to guide the future development of the EU-Asia relations into the coming decade: we must focus on strengthening the EU's political presence across the region'.[67] This statement underlines the desire (if not the ambition) of the EU to become a global actor, and make its presence felt around the world. External relations, in general, and interregionalism, in particular, are also the means for the EU to strengthen its position and compete with other major powers. The European Commission underlines that a key objective of the EU's foreign policy and external relations is to defend its 'legitimate economic and commercial interests in the international arena'.[68] In his study of the EU's relationship with MERCOSUR, Santander concludes that one of the main reasons behind the EU's link with MERCOSUR is to compete with and balance against the US in Latin America and globally.[69]

However, as Söderbaum *et al.* emphasise, a key, if not *the* key objective of the EU foreign policy, in general and interregionalism, in particular, is to promote liberal internationalism, which is the liberal and civilian underpinnings of the EU.[70] These principles include peace and reconciliation, democracy, the rule of law, respect for human rights, liberty, equality and solidarity. Indeed, many official documents and proclamations issued by the EU's institutions underline these principles and values.[71] Issues, which are strongly emphasised, are human right and democracy, the promotion of which is considered the cornerstone of the EU's foreign policies. That is, 'the pursuit of human rights has become a transversal objective of all the EU's external activities'.[72] Because of this emphasis, in nearly all of its agreements with single countries or regional groupings, especially with those from Africa, Asia and South America, the EU seeks to incorporate a 'human right clause' and democratic conditionality. There are now more 120 such agreements, which underline that normative and liberal principles, in general, and human rights and democratic principles, in particular, play a vital role in the EU's external policies. Indeed, some suggest that the EU feels a moral obligation to promote human rights and 'interfere in the domestic politics of other countries'.[73]

Given these rationales behind the efforts of regional groupings/actors to establish interregional relationships, the question is whether they can achieve their objectives and if so, under what conditions. In addressing this question Doidge introduced the concept of 'actorness'.[74] This consists of three fundamental components: the ability to set goals, the ability to make decisions in relation to these goals, and the ability to pursue policy decided in relation to said goals.[75] He also emphasised that the extent to which interregional relationships matter depends on the level of the actorness of regional actors/groupings involved. This is because 'the level of actorness of regional organization (…) will significantly affect the shapes of interregional dialogues'.[76] In furthering the work of Rüland on the five functions of interregionalism, (see above),[77] Doidge maintains that 'the level of actorness of regional groupings involved in any inter- or transregional dialogue or process will effect the extent to which, and the manner in which, the five deduced functions of such dialogues are performed'.[78]

In summary, there are certain common factors that encourage or force regional organisations and their respective member states to establish interregional arrangements. First, interregionalism is a way for them to compete with or/and protect their economic interests vis-à-vis other major powers. Second, regional actors/groupings use interregionalism to strengthen their presence and identity so that they are recognised in the international arena. Third, regionalism is seen as a means for them to manage the complex interdependence brought about by globalisation. Nonetheless, in addition to these three common features, each region has also its own objectives or strongly focuses on a particular objective when establishing interregionalism because different issues and themes receive different attention in different region. This is exemplified by the EU's use of interregionalism as a way to promote its liberal and normative values. Thus, there is no doubt that actorness, that is the capacity of a regional actor to act, is undoubtedly a significant factor determining the importance (or impact) of interregional relationships. Yet, it seems that the convergence or divergence of values/interests of regional actors also plays a role in defining whether regional actors/groupings can (or fail to) come together and forge significant interregional relationships with each other. The following sections will examine some concrete interregional relationships, exploring why they are established, and their importance in the global system, and under what conditions they become an important layer in the global system.

3.3. Some major interregional relationships

ASEAN-EU relationship and the Asia-Europe Meeting

Informal relations between ASEAN and the EU began in 1972 through the Special Coordinating Committee of ASEAN. Three years later, a joint EC-ASEAN Study Group was established to explore the possibility of establishing cooperation between the two blocs. The first meeting among the permanent representatives of the EC member states, the Commission and the ASEAN ambassadors to the EC was held in 1977. Following those initial and informal contacts, the ASEAN-EC Ministerial

Meeting was officially launched in Brussels on 20 and 21 November 1978. This is considered the real date of birth of interregionalism because it was the first time that an interregional cooperation was formalised between two regional organisations. In 1980, both sides signed a Cooperation Agreement.[79]

The factors that lay behind the formalisation of ASEAN-EU relations included both mutual economic interests and linkages that dated from the colonial period. All ASEAN members, except Thailand, were European colonies. The Preamble of the Agreement emphasised that both sides wanted to consolidate, deepen and diversify commercial and economic cooperation. However, it was the political and security concerns, or more exactly the communist threat that encouraged both sides to strengthen their cooperation. Both blocs were born in the context of the Cold War and were anti-communist. Their relationship was reinforced during the two years leading to the signing of the Agreement by the Soviet-backed Vietnamese invasion of Cambodia (1978) and the Soviet invasion of Afghanistan (1979) because the Soviet threat was perceived to pose a serious concern for two regions and it helped to galvanise their cooperation.[80] This common concern led both sides to strengthen their cooperation in order to contain or balance growing Soviet influence in Europe and Southeast Asia. The EC diplomatically supported and defended ASEAN's position, particularly in the United Nations (UN). Indeed, from 1979 to 1984, ASEAN and the EC voted as a bloc at the UN General Assembly in support of calls for Soviet withdrawal from Afghanistan and

Vietnamese withdrawal from Cambodia. Thus, at the political level, the cooperation between the two blocs was strong and successful.[81] In contrast, until the early 1990s, at the economic level, the ASEAN-EC relationship was essentially a donor-recipient paradigm, in which the ASEAN countries were in a weaker bargaining position or considered as junior partners.

The end of the Cold War opened a new phase in the ASEAN-EC/EU relationship. The new situation provided both sides with great opportunities to renew their cooperation by moving from the traditional recipient-donor paradigm to a more balanced relationship. In the aftermath of the Cold War, ASEAN states agreed to establish the ASEAN Free Trade Area (AFTA) and two other wider regional forums, the Asia-Pacific Economic Cooperation (APEC) and the ASEAN Regional Forum (ARF). ASEAN states also witnessed a period of rapid economic growth. These economic and diplomatic successes made ASEAN more confident and assertive and enabled it to play a more important role in the region. Meanwhile the transformation of the European Community into the European Union allowed it to establish a common foreign and security policy (CFSP) and a single currency and play a global role. Viewed in this new context, there was a need to redefine the 1980 Cooperation Agreement by establishing a closer and more balanced relationship. In the eyes of the ASEAN's leaders, forging a stronger relationship with a robust EU and increasing its involvement in their region, could enable them to counterbalance the role of both the US and China.[82] For the EU, a closer relationship with

ASEAN could enhance its position and presence in East and Southeast Asia.

At the economic level, the 1980 Cooperation Agreement no longer reflected the relations between the two blocs. During the 1980s, ASEAN countries were supplicants, demanding better access for products and trade. By the early 1990s, ASEAN had become the world's tenth largest exporter and developed a trade surplus with the EU. Between the signing of the Agreement and the mid-1990s, trade between the two blocs had increased by more than 470%.[83] In 2002, ASEAN-EU trade represented 5.1% of total world trade; and the EU became ASEAN's third largest trading partner, accounting for 14% of ASEAN trade.[84] Thus, 'greater equality and mutual respect are called for if the EU is to have a positive relationship with ASEAN'.[85]

In contrast to the burgeoning post-Cold War economic relationship, political aspects of ASEAN-EU relations deteriorated during the early 1990s. During the Cold War period, there were few political disagreements of substance between the two sides. This is partly because controversial issues were kept off agenda as the Cold War context reduced the differences and disagreements between the two sides. However, without a shared adversary, causes of friction in the EU-ASEAN emerged. Moreover, the transformation of the EC into the EU brought with it a new mission, which focused on the defence of the European values, including human and fundamental rights, democracy and environmental issues. The promotion of these values became a prominent feature of EU foreign policy and led to a feeling that this obliged it to interfere into the domestic affairs of other countries. By doing so in its interaction vis-à-vis ASEAN states, the EU violated a core, if not *the* cardinal, principle of ASEAN, which is non-interference. Disputes between two sides over the issues of human rights, notably the abuse of human rights in Myanmar and by Indonesia in East Timor, in particular, soured the relationship. This has underlined that ASEAN and EU have different – and, to a certain degree, opposing – agendas and values. Such differences, which were considered as 'value-system friction' between ASEAN and the EU or 'the dark side' of their relationship, were at the heart of their difficulties at renewing the relationship.[86]

In an effort to offer a way out of a completely deadlocked situation, the Singaporean Prime Minister Goh Chok Tong successfully proposed the establishment of the Asia-Europe Meeting (ASEM),[87] which held its first meeting in Bangkok in 1996.[88] However, it can be argued that ASEM was also established to bridge what is called the 'missing link' or 'weak leg' in the triangular relationship between North America, Europe (EU) and East Asia. In this view, ASEM was designed to acknowledge East Asia as the third pillar of the emerging world order, to check and balance the dominating influence of the US, and to prevent the forming of coalitions between two of the regions to the detriment of the third.[89] ASEM was also aimed at promoting open regionalism and building a regional collective identity in East Asia. In addition, ASEM was intended to foster the CFSP of the EU and reinforce a European identity in its relations with the outside world. However, even though ASEAN and the EU sought to overcome their disagreements over the human rights, such sensitive and controversial issues sometimes overshadow the ASEM summits. At the second ASEM in London in 1998, the UK did not grant any visas for Myanmar officials. Given this absence, ASEAN states threatened to boycott the meeting. The crisis and human rights abuse in East Timor overshadowed the third meeting held in Seoul in 2000. The Myanmar issue returned and dominated the meeting in Hanoi in 2004.

In short, even though the ASEAN-EU relationship was often considered the 'corner-stone' of the EU's interaction with all Asian countries, it could not move from a rhetoric or consultative level to a more substantive one.[90] That is, despite being seen as a potential pillar of the new international order, 'the relationship fell well short of new expectations on both sides'.[91] At the heart of the difficulties in their attempt to forge a more substance interregional partnership is the continuing 'value-system friction'. With regard to ASEM, its achievements are modest after twelve years and seven summits (Bangkok – 1996, London – 1998, Seoul – 2000, Copenhagen – 2002, Hanoi – 2004, Helsinki – 2006, and Beijing – 2008). It cannot go beyond information-sharing level and has failed to develop into substantive cooperation. ASEM does not even perform as the balancer, for which it was created. This is partly because of the lack of the actorness on the part of the EU and, even more of the Asian components of ASEM, which have not yet integrated enough to act as a single entity.

In addition, as the issue of human rights shows, the lack of the convergence of values and objectives undermines cooperation between Asia and Europe. Indeed, some observers questioned the possibility of effective Asia-Europe cooperation and asked 'to what extent cooperation can be successful between two regions that do not share the same values and base their cooperation on weak institutional frameworks'.[92]

Despite these setbacks, there are certain positive signs and achievements in the ASEAN-EU relationship, and the ASEM in particular, especially since the turn of the century. In 2003 the European Commission issued an important document, 'A New Partnership with Southeast Asia', in which it emphasised that the EU wanted to forge a strong comprehensive partnership with ASEAN. More recently, both sides decided to start negotiations towards a free trade agreement. Within the context of ASEM, important global issues are discussed. At the fourth meeting in 2002 in Copenhagen, which was the first ASEM meeting after the 9/11 events, both sides strongly focussed on international terrorism and security issues. Similarly, at the last meeting in Beijing in 2008, given the global financial crisis, it was the financial cooperation that dominated the meeting agenda.

The EU – MERCOSUR

The Community's first formal links with regional groups in Latin America can be traced back to the 1970s. However, it was not until the 1990s that the EU adopted a strategy for all of Latin America and the Caribbean. Chief among the interregional arrangements that the EU has established with the regional blocs in the region are its links with MERCOSUR.

Between 1991 and 1994 a number of agreements between the two sides was concluded such as the Inter-institutional Cooperation Agreement in 1992 and the Joint Declaration in 1994, which eventually led to the signing of the EU-MERCOSUR Interregional Framework for Cooperation Agreement (EMIFCA) in Madrid in 1995.[93] What are the rationales behind the rapprochement between the two blocs? First, cultural and historical links played an important role because it is was Portugal and Spain that strongly advocated this rapprochement. The EMIFCA was signed during the EU presidency of Spain.[94] Second, the establishment of relations between the two blocs was also aimed at strengthening the processes of economic liberalisation and democratisation in MERCOSUR countries. The Framework Agreement of 1995, which includes a democratic clause and a political dialogue, is an example of this. Unlike the EU-ASEAN relationship, in the EU-MERCOSUR relationship, not only do both sides 'set the condition that a state must be democratic in order to join; both project through their external relations, especially with their neighbours, the fundamental values that legitimate their own integration process'.[95] The third, and perhaps most important, factor is economic interests. One of the three key pillars set by the EMIFCA is to strengthen economic and commercial cooperation between the two sides. This has been very successful, especially for the European side, with the flows of private capital and commercial trade increased dramatically, making the EU the leading investor and trading partner of MERCOSUR, even replacing the US.

Another important factor or more exactly an actor that pushed MERCOSUR and the EU to foster this interregional relationship is the US. Contrary to the EU, which strongly advocates regional projects in general, and MERCOSUR, in particular, the US seeks to destabilise MERCOSUR. This is because the US views MERCOSUR with suspicion, considering it a barrier and a real opponent to its pan-American free trade initiative, FTAA. That is why, for MERCOSUR and its leading member, Brazil, in particular, the EMIFCA not only consolidated their contact with the EU and provided formal recognition of MERCOSUR as an international entity but also gave it a useful instrument in its strategy towards the US. For Brazil, MERCOSUR is seen as a political and economic alliance to confront other powers, in particular the US in the FTAA and WTO. In a region 'that easily veers towards US hegemony, Brazil as dissenting autonomous voice in Latin America is less effective than a Brazil as a leader of a regional alliance'.[96] For the EU, it was aware of the threat posed by the US project to its strategy of rapprochement with Asia, Latin America and, of course, MERCOSUR. Because of this fear, it had no choice but to strengthen its relations with MERCOSUR, where its enterprises capture 60% of the investment.[97] In addition, both the EU and MERCOSUR share a common view that is to build a multilateral system, which would be an alternative world order to the unilateral and unipolar one that the US has developed in the aftermath of the 9/11 events. However, the multipolar and multilateral world order they seek to build is not one that is built on/around the national major powers, that is the US, China, Japan, Russia, India, and Brazil, but rather one built on/around a network of institutionalised regional groupings, that is a multilateral system based on multiregionalism.

However, in this process of rapprochement, both sides have experienced difficulties. Chief among these is the issue of trade deficit. Even though the trade structures of MERCOSUR and the EU have some significant complementarities, MERCOSUR faces a major deficit in its trade with the EU. One of the key reasons for this is the EU's protection of its agricultural products such that South American agricultural exports to the European market face serious obstacles. That also explains why both sides fail to agree to establish a FTA despite more than ten years of negotiations.

The EU and NAFTA

Quite different from the its relations with regional groupings in Asia (ASEAN and ASEM), Latin America (MERCOSUR) or its partnerships with Southern Mediterranean or African groupings, the EU's links with North America is bilateral in form. In other words, the EU has not established an interregional relationship with NAFTA as a whole, but rather with its individual members, with which the EU either institutionalised commercial relations (the US and Canada) or established free trade agreement (Mexico). That is the reason why a free trade agreement between the two groups has not been established. There are different factors explaining the absence of interregional relationship between the two blocs.

One of the key reasons is NAFTA's lack of institutional structure. While the EU is an economic union, with a powerful commission, NAFTA is simply a free trade area, which does not have any executive with the external negotiating power similar to the European Commission. However, the most important reason may be the US's overall non-preference for regionalism. While the EU seeks to create a network of interregional arrangements, in full accordance with its regionalist ideology, the US does not values regional relations, and only enters into regional projects when it cannot operate without doing so.[98]

In addition, according to Aggarwal and Fogarty, there are three factors that explain the limits of interregionalism between the EU and North America.[99] First, the transatlantic free trade area (TAFTA) does not bring potential gains. Second, they argue that both the EU and US have developed strategies to secure export markets for their producers. For the EU, for instance, as a primarily civilian power, commercial policy is its most effective means of exercising international influence. Establishing trade links with other regional groupings is a way for them to practice this influence. In most cases, the EU is in the dominant position, which allows it to dictate the terms/rules of interregional agreements. However, in its relationship with North America, the EU cannot set the rules. Finally, the divergences (of views and ways of working) between the EU and the US also prevent both sides from establishing the TAFTA. Chief among these is that the two sides have different social models. While one opts for a more centralised approach while the other is dominated by *laissez faire* capitalism. With regard to their approaches to the global affairs, one prefers 'soft power' and multilateralism, the other champions 'hard power' and unilateralism.

4. Conclusion: Impact of regionalism and interregionalism

From what has been said above, some important conclusions can be drawn. First, since the end of the Cold War, regional groupings of varying kinds and forms have been estalished in almost every part of the world. Almost all countries, rich and developed as well as poor and developing, have sought to initiate or join at least one of these regional groupings. Second, even though the forms, objectives and approaches of regional projects differ significantly, countries participate for a rather limited range of reasons. That is, they seek to further their influence, to avoid being marginalised in a world, which is both globalised and regionalised or to counter the uncertainties and risks that a volatile global capital market can bring about. The latter become significantly more important in the wake of the 1997 financial crises in Asia and Latin America. As Hurrell has suggested, the 'region is the most appropriate and viable level to reconcile the changing and intensifying pressures of global capitalist competition on the one hand with the need for political regulation and management on the other'.[100] Third, it should be stressed that there are certain cases in which 'engaging in regionalism is just doing what others do', and many of these projects have achieved little.[101] This is particularly apparent in Africa, where the rhetoric of cooperation has hardly translated into substantive cooperation. Despite this, it is widely recognised that regionalism is playing an increasing role in shaping the world order. Regional groupings increasingly seek to play an important role in the global system, and are a key element in the trend towards a multipolar world.

With regard to the EU, even though it has faced certain difficulties in its process of integration, such as the constitutional crisis, or the lack of strong CFSP, it has emerged as a prominent world actor. In economic terms, it is the biggest and strongest pillar of the world's triad. It is also an important force, if not *the* most important, in dealing with climate change, promoting development cooperation, regional integration, human rights and democracy. With regard to security, while the lack of a strong and unified policy continues to undermined the EU's position, it has dared to challenge the US's unilateralism.

Other regional groupings have also challenged the US and its dominance, at least in terms of economic weight and political impact. This is demonstrated in South America and East Asia, by the South American Community of Nations and the East Asian Community. The US is purposively excluded from the new forums such as ASEAN Plus Three or the East Asian Summit. Indeed, it should be stressed that in many cases interregional projects were established, at least in part, to counter the predominance of the US. For example, behind the ASEM is the felt need by European and Asian partners to relate to, and try to balance, the US dominance. More broadly, it can be argued that interregionalism is designed to build a world order that provides an alternative to the unilateral and unipolar one promoted by the US since the end of the Cold War, and particularly under the George B. Bush administration in the aftermath of the 9/11 event. This world order would be regulated by international rules that are as widely accepted as possible. Such a system may be expected to be based on multipolarity and multilateralism, with regional blocs and their interregional relationships playing a prominent role. In other words, in this post-Westphalian world order, the state system would be replaced or complemented by a regionalised world order.

However, building such a 'Pax Europaea', based on interregionalism and multiregionalism, as favoured by the EU, and as an alternative to 'Pax Americana' remains a utopian vision. Nevertheless, that does not mean it is impossible. Such a multilateral agenda seems to be more urgent and has more chance of implementation, given the US's failure in Iraq and in its war on terrorism in general.[102] Building such a world order will necessitate a shift in US foreign policy from unilateralism to multilateralism, which perhaps is more likely to happen under the Barack Obama administration. In addition, the regional actors must not only increase their actorness, but also converge their values, perceptions, interests and approaches. As the ASEAN-EU relationship proves, these two requirements are essential for the establishment of strong interregional relationships that can make a real impact on the world order.

Finally, looking back on world affairs since the end of the Cold War, regionalism, despite, in some respects its still limited results, can be argued to have become an 'indelible feature of the international system',[103] and 'an important dynamic in world politics of the 1990s and will remain one into the new millennium'.[104] Given their proliferation and growing importance, regionalism and interregionalism may be the critical elements in the route to a multilateral and multipolar world order.

Notes

1   Paolo Subacchi, 'Introduction', *International Affairs*, vol. 84 (3), 2008, p. 413.

2   Francis Fukuyama, 'Is America Ready for a Post-American World?', *New Perspective Quarterly*, Fall issue, 2008, p. 42.

3   *Global Trends 2025: A Transformed World*. Available at http://www.dni.gov/nic/PDF_2025/2025_Global_Trends_Final_ Report.pdf [accessed on 10 October 2009].

4   Fareed Zakaria, 'Facing a Post-American World', *New Perspective Quarterly*, Summer issue, 2008, p. 7.

5   Parag Khanna, 'Here Comes the Second World', *New Perspective Quarterly*, Summer issue, 2008, p. 13.

6   Andrew Hurrell, 'One World? Many Worlds? The Place of Regions in the Study of International Society', *International Affairs*, vol. 83 (1), 2007, p. 130.

7   Mary Farrell, 'The Global Politics of Regionalism: An Introduction', in Mary Farrell *et al.* (eds), *Global Politics of*

Regionalism: Theory and Practice, Pluto Press, London, 2005, p. 1.

8 George Howard Joffé, 'Preface', in Mario Telò (ed.), *European Union and New Regionalism: Regional Actors and Global Governance in a Post-Hegemonic Era*, 2nd ed. Ashgate Publishing, Hampshire and Burlington , 2007, p. xiii.

9 Vinod K. Aggarwal and Edward A. Fogarty, 'The Limit of Interregionalism: The EU and North America', *European Integration*, vol. 27 (3), 2005, p. 327.

10 Ibid.

11 Peter Dicken, *Global Shift: Making the Changing Contour of the World Economy*, 5th ed. Sage Publications, London, 2007, p. 189.

12 Francesco Duina, 'Varieties of Regional Integration: The EU, NAFTA and Mercosur', *European Integration*, vol. 27 (3), 2005, p. 247.

13 Farrell, *loc. cit.*, p. 8.

14 Donald Barry and Ronald Keith, 'Introduction: Changing Perspectives on Regionalism and Multilateralism', in Donald Barry and Ronald Keith (eds), *Regionalism, Multilateralism, and the Politics of Global Trade*, University of Columbia Press, Vancouver, 2000, p. 3.

15 It is often argued that regional groupings such as ASEAN and the EEC were formed independently to promote regional cooperation. Such an argument is, to a certain degree, true. However, the backup and stimulation from the US behind these organisations are significantly important.

16 Farrell, *loc. cit.*, p. 2.

17 Andrew Hurrell, 'The Regional Dimension in International Relations Theory', in Farrell *et al.* (eds), *op. cit.*, p. 42.

18 Helen Nesadurai, 'The Global Politics of Regionalism: Asia and the Asia-Pacific', in Farrell *et al.* (eds), *op. cit.*, pp. 155-170.

19 Farrell, *loc. cit.*, p. 16.

20   Martin Rhodes and Richard Higgott, 'Introduction: Asian Crises and the Myth of Capitalist "Convergence"', *The Pacific Review*, vol. 13 (1), 2000, pp. 15-16.

21   Farrell, *loc. cit.*, p. 8.

22   Pier Carlo Padoan, 'The Political Economy of New Regionalism and World Governance', in Telò (ed.), *op. cit.*, p. 53.

23   Tie Jun Zhang, 'Towards Regional Actor and World Player', in Farrell *et al.* (eds), *op. cit.*, pp. 237-251.

24   Björn Hettne, 'Interregionalism and World Order: The Diverging EU and US Models', in Telò (ed.), *op. cit.*, pp. 112-113.

25   Björn Hettne, 'Beyond the 'New' Regionalism', *New Political Economy*, vol. 10 (4), 2005, p. 561.

26   Ibid.

27   Thomas Christiansen, 'European Integration and Regional Cooperation', in John Baylis and Steve Smith (eds), *The Globalization of World Politics: An Introduction to International Relations*, 3rd ed. Oxford University Press, Oxford, 2005, p. 587-588.

28   Ibid.

29   Charles A. Kupchan, 'The New Transatlantic Interregionalism and the End of the Atlantic Alliance', in Heine Hänggi *et al.* (eds), *Interregionalism and International Relations: A Stepping Stone to Global Governance?*, Routledge, London, 2006, p. 146.

30   Charlotte Bretherton and John Vogler, *The European Union as a Global Actor*, Routledge, London and New York, 1999; 2006.

31   Jan Zielonka, 'Europe as a Global Actor: Empire by Example', *International Affairs*, vol. 84 (3), 2008, p. 474.

32   Robert Kagan, *Of Paradise and Power: America and Europe in the New World Order*, Alfred A. Knopf, New York, 2003; 2004.

33   The notion of 'civilian power' was first termed by Francois Duchêne, 'Europe's Role in World Peace', in Richard Mayne (ed.),

Europe Tomorrow: Sixteen Europeans Look Ahead, Fontana, London, 1972. The term of 'normative power' is used by Ian Manners, 'Normative Power Europe: A Contradiction in Terms?', *Journal of Common Market Studies*, vol. 40 (2), 2002, pp. 235-258.

34 The inaugural meeting of the ARF was held in July 1994 in Bangkok; and the 18 participants were: the ASEAN-Five, the US, Australia, China, the EU, India, Japan, Laos, New Zealand, Papua New Guinea, Russia, South Korea, the US and Vietnam.

35 Anthony S. Smith, 'ASEAN's Ninth Summit: Solidifying Regional Cohesion, Advancing External Linkages', *Contemporary Southeast Asia*, vol. 26 (3), 2004, p. 421.

36 Sheldon Simon, 'ASEAN and Multilateralism: The Long, Bumpy Road to Community', *Contemporary Southeast Asia*, vol. 30 (2), 2008, p. 281.

37 Mohan Malik, 'The East Asia Summit', *Australian Journal of International Affairs*, vol. 60 (2), 2006, p. 207.

38 Rajaram Panda, 'India and the East Asian Community Concept', *Japanese Studies*, vol. 26 (1), 2006, pp. 29-36.

39 Nesadurai, *loc. cit.*, p. 168.

40 Sunhyuk Kim and Yong Wook Lee, 'New Asian Regionalism and the United States: Constructing Regional Identity and Interests in the Politics of Inclusion and Exclusion', *Pacific Focus*, vol. 19 (2), 2004, p. 185.

41 Mark Beeson, *Regionalism, Globalization and East Asia: Politics, Security and Economic Development*, Palgrave, Basingtoke, 2007, p. 217.

42 See Yeo Lay Hwee, 'Japan, ASEAN, and the Construction of an East Asian Community', *Contemporary Southeast Asia*, vol. 28 (2), 2006, pp. 259-275; and Takashi Terada, 'Forming an East Asian Community: A Site for Japan-China Power Struggle, *Japanese Studies*, vol. 26 (1), 2006, pp. 5-17.

43 Alberta M. Sbragia, 'European Union and NAFTA', in Tèlo (ed), *op. cit.*, pp. 156-157.

44 Gary Hufbauer and Jefferey J. Schott, 'NAFTA's Bad Rap', *The International Economy*, Summer issue, 2008, p. 19.

45 Kelly Diep, 'Waving Amigos: The Politics of American Integration', *Harvard International Review*, Spring issue, 2008, p. 9.

46 Hufbauer and Schott, *loc. cit.*, p. 19.

47 Diep, *loc. cit.*, p. 10.

48 Sbragia, *loc. cit.*, p. 155.

49 Vinod K. Aggarwal and Edward A. Fogarty, 'The Limit of Interregionalism: The EU and North America', *European Integration*, vol. 27 (3), 2005, p. 333.

50 Michael Mecham, 'MERCOSUR: A Failing Development Project', *International Affairs*, vol. 79 (2), 2003, p. 369.

51 Donald G. Richards, 'Dependent Development and Regional Integration: A Critical Examination of the Southern Common Market', *Latin American Perspectives*, vol. 24 (6), 1997, p. 149.

52 Stefan Schirm, 'Hemispheric Interregionalism: Power, Domestic Interests, and Ideas in the Free Trade Area of the Americas (FTAA)', in Hänggi *et al.* (eds), *op. cit.*, p. 272.

53 Mecham, *loc. cit.*, p. 377.

54 Sebastian Santander, 'The European Partnership with MERCOSUR: A Relationship Based on Strategic and Neo-liberal Principles', *European Integration*, vol. 27 (3), 2005, p. 297.

55 Aggarwal and Fogarty, *loc. cit.*, pp. 333-334.

56 Mario Telò, 'Between Trade Regionalization and Various Paths towards Deeper Cooperation', in Telò (ed.), *op. cit.*, p. 143.

57 Carolyn Jenkins, *Catch-up and Convergence: Regional Integration in Southern Africa*, 2003, p. 5. Available at http://tcdc.undp.org/coopsouth/2003-2/CoopSouth_E-8-22.pdf [accessed on 10 October 2009].

58 Abdulla Baabood, 'Dynamics and Determinants of the GCC States' Foreign Policy, with Special Reference to the EU', The Review of International Affairs, vol. 3 (2), 2003, pp. 254-282.

59 Heine Hänggi, 'Interregionalism as a Multifaceted Phenomenon: In Search of a Typology', in Hänggi *et al.* (eds), *op. cit.*, pp. 31-62.

60 Jürgen Rüland, *ASEAN and the European Union: A Bumpy Interregional Relations*. A discussion paper presented at Center for European Integration Studies, 2001, pp. 6-8. Available at http://www.zei.de/download/zei_dp/dp_c95_rueland.pdf (accessed on 10 October 2009).

61 Ralf Roloff, 'Interregionalism in Theoretical Perspective: A State of the Art', in Hänggi *et al.* (eds), *op. cit.*, p. 24.

62 Kupchan, *op. cit.*, pp. 131-148.

63 Christopher Dent, 'The Asia-Europe Meeting (ASEM) Process: Beyond the Triadic Political Economy?', in Hänggi *et al.* (eds), *op. cit.*, pp. 113-129.

64 Julie Gilson, 'New Interregionalism? The EU and East Asia', *European Integration*, vol. 27 (3), 2005, pp. 307-326.

65 Martin Holland, '"Imagined" Interregionalism: Europe's Relations with African, Caribbean and Pacific States (ACP)', in Hänggi *et al.* (eds), *op. cit.*, pp. 254-271.

66 Fredrik Söderbaum *et al.*, 'The EU as a Global Actor and the Dynamics of Interregionalism: A Comparative Analysis', *European Integration*, vol. 27 (3), 2005, pp. 365-380.

67 European Communication, *Europe and Asia: Strategic Framework for Enhanced Partnerships*, Communication from the Commission, 2001, p. 15. Available at http://ec.europa.eu/development/icenter/ repository/strategy_asia_2001_en.pdf [accessed on 10 October 2009].

68 European Commission, *A World Player: The European Union's External Relations*, DG for Press and Communication, July 2004,

p. 3. Available at http://bookshop.europa.eu/eubookshop/download.action?fileName=NA5904548ENC_002.pdf&eubphfUid=10059835&catalogNbr=NA-59-04-548-SL-C [accessed on 10 October 2009].

69 Santander, *loc. cit.*, pp. 285-306.

70 Söderbaum *et al.*, *loc. cit.*, pp. 368-370.

71 For instance, in its *Furthering Human Rights and Democracy Across the Globe*, published in 2007, p. 5, the European Commission clearly stated that '[t]he European Union has made human rights and democracy a central aspect of its external relations: in the political dialogue its holds with third countries; through its development cooperation and assistance; or through its action in multilateral fora'. Available at http://ec.europa.eu/external_relations/human_rights/docs/brochure07_en.pdf [accessed on 10 October 2009].

72 Richard Balme, 'The European Union, China and Human Rights', in Zaki Laïdi (ed.), *EU Foreign Policy in a Globalized World: Normative Power and Social Preferences*, Routledge, London and New York, 2008, p. 144.

73 Joergen Oerstroem Moeller, 'ASEAN's Relations with the European Union: Obstacles and Opportunities', *Contemporary Southeast Asia*, vol. 29 (3), 2007, p. 474.

74 Mathew Doidge, *"East is East ..." Inter- and Transregionalism and the EU-ASEAN Relationship*, Doctoral Thesis, University of Canterbury, Christchurch, 2004; 'Inter-regionalism and Regional Actors: The EU-ASEAN Example', in Wim Stokhof *et al.* (eds), *The Eurasian Space: Far More Than Two Continents*, ISEAS Publications, Singapore, 2004, pp. 39-57; 'Joined at the Hip: Regionalism and Interregionalism', *European Integration*, vol. 29 (2), 2007, pp. 229-248; 'Regional Organizations as Actors in International Relations: Interregionalism and Asymmetric

Dialogues', in Jürgen Rüland *et al.* (eds), *Asia-Europe Relations: Building Blocs for Global Governance*, Routledge, Oxon, 2008, pp. 32-54.

75 In their investigation the EU's external relations, Bretherton and Vogler identify not three but five requirements for actorness. They are: (1) shared commitment to a set of overarching shared values and principles; (2) the ability to identify policies priorities and formulate coherent policies; (3) the ability to negotiate effectively with other actors in the international system; (4) the availability of, and capability to employ, policy instruments; and (5) domestic legitimating of decision processes, and priorities relating to external policy. See Bretherton and Vogler, *op. cit.*, p. 38.

76 Doidge, 'Inter-regionalism and Regional Actors', *loc. cit.*, p. 48.

77 Rüland theorises the five functions of interregionalism and then uses the ASEAN-EC/EU relationship, which he considers as the most advanced interregional relationship, as an empirical base to examine the so-called five functions of interregionalism. By doing so, he discovers that the ASEAN-EC/EU relationship barely or only partly performs these five functions. However, he does not go further to explain why that is the case. Taking Rüland's failure as a launching point, Doidge attempts to explain it by injecting the concept of regional actorness

78 Doidge, *"East is East ... "*, *loc. cit.*, p. 11.

79 This Cooperation Agreement was signed in Kuala Lumpur, Malaysia on 7 March 1980. Available at http://www.aseansec.org/1501.htm [accessed on 10 October 2009].

80 Yeo Lay Hwee, 'The Inter-regional Dimension of EU-Asia Relations: EU-ASEAN and the Asia-Europe Meeting (ASEM) Process', *European Studies*, vol. 25, 2007, p. 178.

81 Ibid., pp. 178-179.

82 Susanne Rentzow-Vasu, *Explaining EU-ASEAN Relations under the*

North-South Divide. Paper to be presented at the International Studies Association 2006 Convention, San Diego, p. 8. Available at http://www.allacademic.com/meta/p_mla_apa_research_citation/1/0/0/3/5/p100351_index.html [accessed on 10 October 2009].

83 Magnus Petersson, 'Myanmar in EU-ASEAN Relations', *Asia-Europe Journal*, vol. 4, 2006, p. 573.

84 European Commission, *A New Partnership with Southeast Asia*, Communication for the Commission, 2003, p. 6. Available at http://www.eurosoutheastasia-ict.org/docs/anewpartnership.pdf [accessed on 10 October 2009].

85 Joseph A. McMahon, 'ASEAN and the Asia-Europe Meeting: Strengthening the European Union's Relationship with South-East Asia', *European Foreign Affairs*, vol. 3, 1998, p. 238.

86 See Eero Palmujoki, 'EU-ASEAN Relations: Reconciling Two Different Agendas', *Contemporary Southeast Asia*, vol. 19 (3), 1997, pp. 269-285; Christopher Dent, *The European Union and East Asia: An Economic Relationship*, Routledge, London, 1999, p. 51; Anthony Forster, 'Evaluating the EU-ASEM Relationship: A Negotiated Order Approach', *Journal of European Public Policy*, vol. 7 (5), 2000, p. 791; Jörn Dosch, 'The ASEAN-EU Relations: An Emerging Pillar of the New International Order?', in Suthiphand Chirativat *et al.* (eds), *Asia-Europe on the Eve of the 21st Century*, Centre for European Studies, Bangkok, 2001, p. 64.

87 Forster, *loc. cit.*, p. 795.

88 Contrary to the ASEAN-EC/EU cooperation agreement, the ASEM is a highly informal and non-legally-binding arrangement. It is held in a two-year rotation, and has so far had seven meetings, with the last one, was held in Beijing in October 2008. In addition to the 10 members of ASEAN and 25 members of the EU, it now includes India, Pakistan and Mongolia.

89 Heine Hänggi, 'ASEM and the Construction of the New Triad',

Journal of the Asia Pacific Economy, vol. 4 (1), 1999, p. 57.

90 Moeller, *loc. cit.*, p. 465.

91 Forster, *loc. cit.*, p. 795.

92 Petersson, *loc. cit.*, p. 576.

93 Claudia Sanchez Bajo, 'The European Union and Mercosur: A Case of Inter-regionalism', *Third World Quarterly*, vol. 20 (5), 1999, p. 931.

94 Andy Klom, 'Mercosur and Brazil: A European Perspective', *International Affairs*, vol. 79 (2), 2003, pp. 352-53

95 Alvaro Vasconcelos, 'European Union and MERCOSUR', in Telò (ed.), *op. cit.*, p. 171.

96 Klom, *loc. cit.*, p. 352.

97 Santander, *loc. cit.*, p. 293.

98 Hettne, 'Interregionalism and World Order', *loc. cit.*, p. 118.

99 Aggarwal and Fogarty, *loc. cit.*, pp. 335-340.

100 Hurrell, 'The Regional Dimension in International Relations Theory', *loc. cit.*, pp. 42-43.

101 Louise Fawcett, 'Regionalism from an Historical Perspective', in Farrell *et al.* (eds), *op. cit.*, p. 31.

102 Vasconcelos, *loc. cit.*, p. 179.

103 Doidge, 'Joined at the Hip: Regionalism and Interregionalism', *loc. cit.*, p. 230.

104 Michael Smith, 'Regions and Regionalism', in Brian White *et al.* (eds), *Issues in Politics*, 3rd ed. Palgrave Macmillan, New York, 2005, p. 68.

www.ingramcontent.com/pod-product-compliance
Lightning Source LLC
Chambersburg PA
CBHW022129280326
41933CB00007B/615